101 Ideas to Kick Your Ass into Gear

101 Ideas to Kick Your Ass into Gear

Ian Gray & Nicklaus Suino

MASTER & FOOL, LLC

Master and Fool, LLC
3853 Research Park Drive, Suite 110
Ann Arbor, Michigan 48104

10 9 8 7 6 5 4 3 2 1

FIRST EDITION

Written, Edited, and Printed in the United States of America

ISBN-13: 978-0615579337

ISBN-10: 0615579337

*To the countless friends and business associates
who have helped us understand that
the journey is the destination,
and that good friends are the ultimate achievement.*

CONTENTS

VISUALIZE

APPENDIX

*There is simply not enough space here
to express our gratitude to the many individuals
who helped support us in this endeavor.
You know who you are.
Thank you.*

Introduction

Thanks to the brilliant engineering behind a few modern inventions - namely the Herman Miller Aeron chair, the personal computer, and the widescreen, Dolby Surround Sound home entertainment center - we spend more time glued to our glutes than ever. The latest numbers suggest that the average person spends sixty hours or more a week using his butt as a base of operations. That makes the objective of this book - unplanting your patootie - that much more difficult; how are we supposed to "kick your ass into gear" if you're SITTING ON IT?

That's why we've presented you with 101 activities ranging from those which would cause any rational person to tremble in fear - like organizing your office - to things that you may consider just an ordinary weekend pastime - like jumping into the abyss with a giant rubber band tied around your waist. This book doesn't spend much time on motivational theory – the danger there is that you may spend more time PONDERING doing things than actually DOING them.

The plan here is to put some dare in your derrière, some juice in your caboose, and some whoosh in your toosh. And to help you get out of the rut created by your butt. As American novelist Ellen Glasgow said, "The only difference between a rut and a grave are the dimensions." So don't worry about doing any of the things we suggest the "right" way, just DO them. When you're strapped to the top of a car going 100 miles an hour down the highway shouting, "Banzaaaaaaaai!" it won't matter much if you're following one of our ideas to the letter. (That's NOT one of our ideas, by the way. What, do you think we're crazy?)

So what are you waiting for? Pick a chapter and put some hum in your bum, some flair in your fanny, and some kick in your can! After you've done a dozen or so of these activities, you'll look back and wonder how you ever managed to spend so much time parked on your posterior.

Highlights

1. Quit

Quit. Quit your job. Quit smoking. Quit eating so much crap food. Quit pining over that lost love from three years ago. Quit saying you're gonna clean out the garage. Quit saying "I'm gonna start working out tomorrow." Quit comparing yourself. Quit watching TV. Quit complaining. Quit while you're ahead. They say quitters never win, but the truth is that knowing when to quit something may be the most winning action you'll ever take. Quit procrastinating, and quit something today. It might rock your world.

2. Tell your story

Who's more likely to do the next great thing, a woman who landed a job in radio in high school and who was co-anchoring the local evening news by age 19, or a woman who was raised by a poor, single, teenage mother and who was raped at the age of nine? Fans of Oprah Winfrey will recognize that they're the same person, but if you only knew one side or the other, you might draw some very wrong conclusions about where the story is going to go.

When you tell your own story, you can have a powerful influence on what the reader believes will come next. By focusing on the times in your life when you were most productive and most positive, you can paint a picture of someone who is going to do great things.

Who's the most important reader of this story? You are! In fact, you tell yourself your own story constantly. Most of the time, you do it unconsciously, so you repeat what you've been telling yourself for years. Try taking conscious control of your story and tell it in a way that makes the next great step inevitable.

3. Buy a really nice pair of sunglasses

Are you the kind of person who cowers behind the revolving sunglasses display at the supermarket, self-consciously sneaking a peek at how you look as you try on sunglasses? I am. Unless I remember how fun it can be. Take a friend if you can, but if you can't, it's almost MORE fun if you ask total strangers to help. You will be absolutely stunned by how helpful most people will try to be. Start with the most absurd pair on the rack. Go for an Elton John or Lady Gaga vibe. Have a laugh, and ham it up. Then try those styles you're always afraid to try because they make too much of a statement.

Everyone should have at least two pairs of sunglasses — one pair that's tasteful enough to wear to a funeral, and one pair that makes a powerful statement. It doesn't matter if the statement is "I am a secret service agent" or "I am a wealthy movie star, please don't ask for my autograph." Next time you're looking for shades, remember that they project as much as they protect.

4. Write a 250-year plan

Did you know that the founder of Matsushita Electronics created a 250-year plan? Most of us worry about what we're going to do tomorrow or next month, and this guy is deciding what his company will be like in two and half centuries! Would you accomplish your goals if you could work on them for 10 years, then do it again and again ... 25 times over? Write a vision of your life in 250 years, then create manageable steps to make it happen. A big part of the fun is just imagining what life will be like in the year 2261!

5. Call the most famous person you can think of

I just tried this myself, and it gave me a lot of adrenaline! I got nowhere close to a famous golfer, left a voicemail for a businessman whose name is a household word, and actually spoke to an aging rock star. I told him how much I like his music, and he seemed happy to hear it. What I came away with was a sense that even the most famous people are no more than a phone call away. If I have the right message I should be able to have a conversation with them.

You know in your heart that's true for you, too. It's rarely competence alone that keeps us from reaching our potential; it's often our lack of confidence. This is a great way to turn your self-limiting ideas upside down!

6. Live blindfolded for twenty-four hours

Yeah, some of you got worked up just reading the heading, didn't you. Well you may find this a little less fun without the fur-lined handcuffs or whatever else you use when you're blindfolded as a leisure pursuit.

I've tried to live blindfolded twice in my life. Trying to move through an ordinary day blindfolded will totally kick your ass in ways you might not have expected. You may find some things easy, then turn around to be surprised to discover how hard it can be to shave when you can't see what you're doing. If you're a man, you may wonder why you shave at all, since you can't see your face.

Things will get a little more exciting when you leave the house. But you also may discover that your senses will attenuate so much that certain things are a lot easier than you expected. Like locating a coffee shop or guessing which way the traffic is moving. And speaking of traffic, driving is one activity we strongly urge you to avoid during this activity.

7. Turn off the phone AND the computer

I can already hear you, in a Darth Vader voice, screaming "NoooooOOOOOOOOOooooo!!!!," but I dare you. Studies show that a disturbing percentage of adults' first activity of the day is checking email, and for younger digital natives, over 70% specifically log onto Facebook first thing. And now that the web is tied to our smartphones with an added frosting of "apps," this reality becomes even more pervasive. And how many times a day do you "Google" something because of poor memory recall?

I dare you. Try it. Just for a day. For some it feels like sensory deprivation torture at first, but you may quickly find yourself talking to the checkout people you usually ignore, or maybe smiling at a stranger and MAKING A REAL LIFE FRIEND or something. Try it. Just for a day. Just don't forget to come back. I've left you like ten voicemails already.

8. Go skydiving

If you found yourself looking through a doorway that looked over a vast expanse of wheat and cornfields, with a hundred mile an hour wind blasting by outside, what would you do? Step through into the abyss? Not me! That's why, on my first jump, I was SHOVED out of the plane. I did this years ago, but these days it's a much more user-friendly pastime. Tandem jumps take away the need for extensive training, and having jumped solo, I GUARANTEE that looking at the world from several thousand feet up while you're rapidly falling toward it will change your perception for a day, if not forever.

9. Go live with the Inuit

You probably think we're joking, but we're not. An acquaintance of mine actually went to live with the Inuit in Greenland for a year, and it changed his life forever in ways that at least HE considered positive. You don't have to be an anthropologist or philanthropist to do this; the fellow in question owned a retail store, and the store is doing better today than before the trip.

I'll never forget how he looked upon his return. His eyes gave you the impression that although he was looking at you, he was also looking THROUGH you. He attributed this to looking at a barren white landscape for a year, but the fact is his OUTLOOK changed too. If you don't like snow, there are plenty of other options. I've always joked that the only way I'd ever get a tattoo is if I earned it in a Maori ritual. Maybe I should kick my ass into gear and do it

10. Give in to greed

You know you want that Kawasaki Ninja ZX. I know I do. But I have this internal conflict because it's such a superficial desire. Shouldn't I want World Peace or something?

Well, I want that, too, but in the meantime, I want a really fast motorcycle. Are you conflicted because you aren't sure you're worthy of the splurge? Trust me, you're splurge-worthy. Fuck it. Print out the motorcycle photo, put it on your bathroom mirror, and work your ass off until you can buy it.

11. Make a bet that you can do it

Having trouble getting started on something? Do you respond well to a challenge? Then make a bet!

In May 1993, over a game of cribbage, I bet my father than I could be admitted to law school by the end of summer. The bet was only five bucks, but once I was committed, there was no way I was going to let myself lose. If you think this might work for you, go to someone whose opinion you value and bet that you can do the thing you've been putting off. Then, whatever it takes, make sure you win the bet!

12. Exploit your kids

Hey, your kids are just taking up space in the house. Might as well put them to some use.

What we actually mean is that you should reflect on what kind of life you want to provide for your kids, and use that as motivation to get your ass in gear. What do you think we are, monsters? If you're like most people, you love your children deeply, and you want the best for them. If you consciously pair those powerful feelings with a step-by-step plan to reach your goals, we suspect you'll be highly motivated. Plus, those little fingers can really sew!

Get Out of Your Comfort Zone

13. Ask someone on a date

This is often one of the most over-pondered and under-pursued activities in the world. Stop pondering, and pursue. The results will be both more rewarding and more boring than you think. You MIGHT discover that the person you've been thinking of asking out is the other half of your wedding cake topper, but face it, the odds of that are extremely unlikely.

On the bright side, you'll either find the person in question has mutual interests with you, or not. And if they DO, repeated proximity allows more opportunities for lightning to strike. And if they DON'T, that's one less irrelevant thing keeping your ass from getting into gear!

14. Go for a balloon ride

Are you afraid of heights? Strangely, flying a couple thousand feet above the ground in a hot air balloon may be one of the best first steps toward overcoming that fear. But make sure you fly with a truly seasoned pilot, preferably in a place like Albuquerque New Mexico, where the terrain and currents are especially suited to a calmer flight.

In good hands, a hot air balloon flight is one of the most serene and calming experiences you will ever experience. I personally ENJOY heights, but the first time I went up, I was with two trembling, bullet-sweating, confirmed acrophobics. But you know what? Once they got over the pre-launch jitters and floated gently up in the air like a....a....BALLOON, their faces were alive with the dazzled eyes and ear-to-ear smiles usually reserved for small children watching parades.

And you know what both of these self-proclaimed panic-stricken flight fearers did after our (slightly bumpy) landing? They asked when they could do it again. And the bumpy landing? In spite of having to maneuver themselves around relative strangers in a large, previously vertical passenger basket that was now lying on its side, one of the previously fearful passengers said "Wow, that was fun! It's like playing 'Twister' without the mat!"

15. Change your hairstyle

Are you the sort of person who doesn't think your hairstyle is especially important? Well, I guess that would explain why you haven't changed it in over a decade! I'd also have to add that you're probably the only one that thinks so. No, most people don't walk around doing mental Glamour Magazine "Don'ts" as they look at other people's hair. But they sure do take notice when someone has a sharp and flattering style, especially if it's a CHANGE in style. As Alec Baldwin's character Jack Donaghy said on the show "30 Rock," "Your hair is your head suit."

16. Get a style makeover

They say that Einstein had at least a full week's supply of the same suit, and that Steve Jobs has literally hundreds of pairs of his trademark black shirt and faded jeans. They both presumably did or do this because it removes a significant mental distraction from their day, i.e., the question "what to wear today?" But unless you're busy outlining the theory of relativity or putting some recent touches on your global domination of the portable digital device markets, maybe it's time for a change in style. If you take pride in the fact that you have your apparel shopping down to a science, remember that even in science, paradigms change.

Some new clothes will not only make an impression on those around you, they literally make you FEEL different. Who doesn't love the lively feeling of a new shirt or a new dress and the way it makes your body feel more alive? If you don't know what I mean, it has DEFINITELY been too long. One little tip: make more than one shopping trip, and on successive trips take someone of each gender. There's nothing like the opinion of the opposite sex, and your same-sex friends will probably be more painfully honest when necessary. For men, the problem may be finding a guy friend who doesn't think this kind of activity is "gay." Here's a tip. Lose those friends. It's the twenty-first century.

17. Learn To swim

If (like me) you don't know how to swim, this should be on the top of your Kick Your Ass list. As a youngster, I never learned to swim mostly because my siblings used the same method to teach ME that our father used to teach THEM, which was "throw the kid off the dock." Except they forgot the part where someone would be in the water to help you out as you floundered, and I nearly drowned.

Oddly, I wasn't left especially traumatized; I just had a low "interest in learning to swim" quotient. As a teen, I learned through a minor boating mishap on Lake Washington that I was capable of not drowning. "Not drowning" is hardly the same as "swimming," but this knowledge let me procrastinate more. Why make a big deal of learning to swim if you know you can survive in hundreds of feet of choppy water? Well, the fact is that swimming is fun, social, and one of the healthiest physical activities you can engage in, and denying yourself all of this is just plain cruel. So I just put this on the top of my list.

18. Sell yourself as an expert, then deliver

For me, this was the first step in starting a successful web consulting career, when in fact I was something of a noob at the time. It's kind of common knowledge in many fields that when a client comes to you and asks "Can you do A, B, and C?" the correct answer is always "Of course! That's one of our specialties!" even if the technology doesn't even exist in the first place.

You then turn around and FIGURE IT OUT. You don't have to lie though, since there's a good chance you're an expert at SOMETHING, even if it's skipping stones on a lake or cat herding. The idea here is to reach out, build the trust required, and then provide both yourself and the client with the incredible satisfaction both enjoy with a challenge met.

19. Check your bank statement

The other day as I was heading to the bank, I ran into a friend who asked where I was going. "To the bank, and I'm laughing all the way," I replied, laughing. I didn't tell them I was depositing 50 bucks to make sure an expense account didn't get overdrawn. Personally, I've always been a little meticulous with reviewing my accounts, but in light of the mini-scandals of certain banks' sneaky charges and dodgy deposit posting practices, checking your bank statement should just be common sense these days.

But another great reason to check your bank statement is to put a fire under your ass. How much is in there that's not already committed to paying for something? A lot? If so, is it just in a standard savings or checking account? MOVE IT! Make it make money. Is there as much as you'd like? SET SOME GOALS FOR CHANGING THAT. One great goal is to have no debt at all, and have all your money making more money. Is that on your "to do" list? I imagine many people DON'T look at their bank statement for the very reason they SHOULD look at it. It doesn't reflect where they'd really like to be. Turn that around. Reality checks don't bounce.

20. Say yes

Did you ever see the movie "Yes Man," in which Jim Carrey's character agrees to a motivational guru's demand that he says "yes" to everything for a day? Do you think you have the guts to try this? This made me bristle at first when I tried it. The very first thing that happened as I walked out of my house that morning was that a local hustler asked me for money. Giving him the dollar was worth the look of shock on his face; he sees me every day, and knows how I feel about his little scam. I'm sure SOMETHING happened in his brain at that moment.

Later in the day, someone of whom I've never been too fond asked me to join him as I walked by the outdoor cafe where he was sitting. I ended up learning he was much more interesting than I had assumed, and as we sat and talked, he introduced me to a friend of theirs that was passing by, a woman I'd been curious about because of her striking personal manner. She and I have since become great friends! Try saying yes all day, just for a day. You never know where you'll end up!

21. Take a vow of silence

Shut up. No really. Shut up. Just for a day. Do you think you could? I'll be honest. I don't think I'll ever do this. I'm pretty sure my head would explode from all the hot air building up. But I hear the results may be surprising. They say you'll (duh) listen more. You'll obviously have to put some rules in place. It's suggested that you don't make exceptions for texting, email, social networking, etc., so you may want to prepare a card that says "I've taken a vow of silence today" and do the same for all your text-based communication.

You know, on second thought, I have to try this. Aside from a certain amount of satisfaction to be had by not having to talk to certain people in my life, there are also certain people I know who would have a FIELD DAY if they could say anything they like to me and not have to hear my thoughts on the topic.

22. Have a good cry

Like many dads from his generation, my dad would say "Laugh, and the world laughs with you. Cry, and I'll give you somethin' to cry ABOUT!" Too bad for them; they had no idea what they were missing. Our busy lives and disrupted communication these days make it harder than ever to just slow down and FEEL something. So, even though I'm totally capable of crying at a wedding or gesture of kindness, I sometimes have a little cry on purpose.

And sometimes resort to a little trick. Music. We all have one or two tunes that will bring a tear to the eye; maybe it's "Hallelujah" or "Llorando," the Spanish version of Roy Orbison's "Crying." Doesn't matter. Whether you need music or not, let 'er rip once in a while. Although studies don't bear out the common belief that crying has physiological benefits, screw science. We all know that spring fresh feeling in the soul after a good eyeball enema.

23. Express your true feelings

Dude, this ain't the 80's, so you don't need to go around acting so macho anymore. If you're still walking around mumbling your feelings like a caveman, you'll be pleasantly surprised that your Man Card won't be revoked if you shake you buddy's hand, look him in the eye, and say, "You know, I really appreciate your friendship."

Don't worry if your eyes cloud up a little (mine always do in these situations). If your friend is worthy of the name, he'll break into a big smile and give you a sincere, manly hug. If you make a habit of expressing yourself warmly and without reservation, you'll be surprised at how many other obstacles fall away.

24. Go to church

Do you hate the idea of going to church? Have you ever asked yourself why? Do you hate the idea of spending time with people who are trying to have a relationship with the almighty? People who gather in fellowship and help one another, people who come together to celebrate the birth of their children and the marriages of their friends? People who mourn the death of their loved ones?

If so, maybe it's time to consider putting aside your cynicism and visiting a few places of worship. Many won't feel right, but if you find one you like it could be a great place. If it helps get you more in touch with the greater forces in the universe, you'll be happily surprised at how well it helps get you moving when you're stuck.

25. Get your portrait taken

What will you look like when you achieve your most important goals? Will you wear a Perry Ellis suit? A better haircut? Buy a Porsche 911 GTS? You can get a "what I'd look like if I made it" portrait taken without dropping Porsche caliber money. A woman I know called a friend with a camera and spent two hours at the BMW dealership taking photos. The salespeople loved it – she's a stunning woman – and she got some beautiful shots. The best one's on her desk and she says it really motivates her to live up to the image!

26. Ask for a job way above your pay grade

We sincerely believe that most people don't set their aspirations high enough. There are probably as many reasons for this as there are people, but two of the most common reasons are that (1) you fear failure, or (2) you've failed once or twice, so you fear failure. But how you respond to your fears can change everything. You can put your head down and do your best to ignore the fact that opportunity awaits, or you can resolve that you may as well fear something that could be highly rewarding. And, when we try for something we don't really think we can get, we tend to get less tied up in it. Go ahead, apply for a job posting that's well over and above what you think you can get. And don't forget to wear your lucky underwear.

27. Shout!

It's a lot less outrageous to keep your frustration bottled up than to let it out. But you play a kind of mind trick on yourself every time you suppress your frustration in an effort to believe that it's not that bad to put off what you should really be doing right now. Listen, every time you do less than your best you slip further behind your potential. You should be deeply, passionately consumed with grabbing everything that life has to offer. Bring that passion right to the front of your consciousness by shouting it out!

"I want it all! I want it now! I WANT SUCCESS, MOTHER FUCKER! I AM THE TRIPLE GREATEST AND I AM COMING TO TAKE WHAT'S MINE!"

28. Get angry

Aren't you tired of coming up with excuses for why you're not more successful? I know I am! I am fed up with the decision to turn on the television when I have unopened mail on my desk. I am worn out from watching people with less innate talent and fewer opportunities than me do more with their businesses and personal lives. I'm really angry with myself for wasting so much money and so many gifts. I hate the fact that I often choose the easier path when the slightly harder path will yield much better results. I'm ashamed that my family has to endure second best when I know I am capable of getting so much more for them. Using this anger I resolve to do more with what I have and to strive to improve my relationship with the world in meaningful ways every single day.

29. Answer the door naked*

Have you ever answered the door naked? You haven't? You don't know what you're missing! If you're like most of us, opening the door to a stranger when you have no trousers on will take you completely out of your comfort zone (not to mention the effect it will have on your visitor). After you close the door, energized, smiling and embarrassed, you may find that you approach things with a new point of view. That, and the fact that you now have a very curious person on the other side of your door may be all you need to get your ass into gear ... and back into some slacks or a skirt!

*Please don't do anything that is illegal or that would put you at risk just because we suggest it in this book!

30. Make a new friend

I stopped into the diner the other week and this very outgoing guy next to me ordered a peanut butter and bacon sandwich. He flirted relentlessly with the waitresses and fired off about 20 blistering emails on his smartphone. I was so intrigued I struck up a conversation with him. Turns out he owns a huge industrial crating and shipping company and a lot of undeveloped land next to our airport. But the most interesting thing about him was that his company volunteers to take missionaries and their belongings all over the world. We stayed in touch, and his inspiration and drive have helped inspire me to make some very profitable core changes to my business.

31. Walk into every store on Main Street and start a conversation

Quit asking, "Which store should I start in?" That's just another way NOT to get your ass into gear. Start anywhere, dang it. Approach somebody in each store and engage them in conversation. You'd be surprised how many people are willing to drop what they're doing and give you their undivided attention if you show real interest in what they're saying.

Whenever I do something like this I seem to meet at least one person who is not only really interesting, but who offer me an insight that really helps kick my ass into gear.

32. Take a job you're sure you'll hate

I know it sounds crazy, but this can be one of the most enjoyable activities on our list. Are you so invested in your job that you worry more than you should?

Will I be good enough? How can I impress my boss? What if I get fired? With these concerns gone, you have tremendous freedom to be yourself. You'll be more relaxed and a lot less worried about showing who you really are. A couple of nice things can happen. You could be surprised by how much you end up liking something you thought you'd hate. And you might find that people really like the real you. That's powerful stuff.

33. Take a concealed weapons class

Guns polarize people, so if this bugs you, just skip it. But if you don't habitually carry a gun (and I don't), doing so will really take you out of your comfort zone. It's kind of like wearing woman's underwear if you're a straight guy, but not as sexy (I don't usually wear women's underwear, either, by the way).

I got my CPL (Concealed Pistol License), and carried my pistol around for a day. It raised my awareness of personal safety, which I'd wanted to accomplish for a long time, and gave me extra energy that I was able to leverage into some serious personal breakthroughs.

Organize

34. Organize

Did you know that there are people who will organize your life for about a thousand dollars a day? Well, let us save you a few thousand dollars. Because all they do is put to work a few basic ideas. Some of this will seem like no-brainer stuff, but if you're so organized, why are you still reading?

Start with a list. What needs to be sorted? List things, and sort the lists into short, medium, and long-term tasks. Also, sort objects in your life into things you currently use, and things you haven't used for six months or more. Box, file or archive things you haven't used for a while, and start a monthly review of things with the goal of eliminating or properly storing and filing less-used items. Eventually (maybe monthly) sort these "dead" files for things you can completely discard.

For ongoing organization, search the web to learn about the 43 folders system, tickler files, and the Noguchi Filing System. There are dozens of books and web sites you can turn to as well, but the fact is, being organized is more about not neglecting than using a specific system.

35. Have a garage sale

Having a good garage sale can be a cathartic experience on the same level as say, college graduation. Or having children. A poorly planned garage sale, on the other hand, can be an exercise in futility comparable to nailing jello to a cat. If you're just doing it because you need money, you might do better by panhandling. But if you treat it as a way to get paid for organizing your house, it can be fun and profitable.

It's amazing how many things we manage to hold onto when we have someplace to put them, but what you may not realize until you start getting rid of this stuff is how much space in your HEAD is freed as you free space in your HOUSE. But be smart, and be real about what will sell. Separate things that are going to be more work to sort and price than they're worth. Like your acid-wash jeans from 1983, and your home-recorded Seinfeld collection on VHS. Likewise, separate things that would fetch more money on Craigslist or eBay.

We're not here to provide a complete garage sale planning guide, but we have one more tip. Have a garden hose ready for the more persistent of the bargain hunters that start showing up at 7am when the posted start time was noon.

36. Set a deadline

This may seem like an obvious thing to kick your ass into gear, but although many of us are great at setting deadlines within some specific work-related project, we forget to do the same thing with our hopes and dreams in "regular" life. Been looking for a partner? Been meaning to make millions of dollars? Been thinking about relocating? GIVE IT A DEADLINE. You'll be amazed how quickly the most seemingly abstract or unattainable goals become a reality once you set a date for them. I personally have a magic whiteboard. Whenever I put something on my whiteboard, it magically happens. Some people say this also works with a sheet of paper or index card that you carry with you and look at daily.

37. Prioritize

Just between you and me, nobody really does this. Except successful people. Or people who are going to be successful. Hint, hint. So, do you really need us to explain how to do it? Okay, here goes: write down all the shit you have to do. Figure out what absolutely needs your attention right now, what can wait a day or a week, and what you should be working on over the long term. Write out the list, from most urgent to least urgent. Then, do the most urgent thing first. When that's done, do the next thing. Wash, rinse, repeat.

38. Get a plan (from somebody who's already done it)

The late Dr. James McConnell, author of Understanding Human Behavior (the best-selling college textbook of its time), was once a mentor of mine. He used to say, "Don't reinvent the wheel. Find a model and start there."

He was right. We spend too much time trying to build things from the ground up. We would save time and agony if we used plans created by people who have already suffered through the invention phase. What do you want to do? Who's done it? What do they say is the best way to go about it? Follow their plan, even if you have to buy it. You may get a lot farther in a whole lot less time.

39. Measure your progress

Listen, you undifferentiated jackwagon, you suffer from a lack of motivation! You keep starting things and running out of steam! I know your type.

Because I am your type. At least I used to be. Then I figured out that I was working too much. T-O-O M-U-C-H. Instead of working so much, I should have been measuring my progress. That way, I'd know how far I'd come from where I started, and how much closer I was to my goals. That would have provided two kinds of motivation: the kind that says "look, sucker, if you don't get your ass into gear, you'll never get this done!" And the kind that says, "hey, lookit how far you've already come! This is gonna be a piece of cake!"

40. Burn it

If you've ever been to a bonfire party, you know how much just a basic bonfire can kick your ass. Flames flying 30 or 40 feet in the air, embers shooting skyward like little reverse meteors. And you may find the day after that you accidentally got a "sunburn." But have you ever had a bonfire party with a PURPOSE? The ritual purpose of burning away the past to free you for the future? This can be incredibly liberating, and you can share the experience with others. In fact, that makes it more fun.

The last time I did this, I have to confess that I kept having the urge to run into my house and burn EVERTHING. But that may be a reflection of where my life was at the time. Just use some common sense and don't burn plastics, batteries, or other toxic materials or explosives. And make sure you're not violating any local ordinances, or you'll get you ass kicked in ANOTHER way, when the cops show up.

Get Physical

41. Climb a wall

You may already be doing this, but cubicle or living room walls don't count. If you feel like climbing a wall, it may be because you're sitting on your butt. Good news! You can keep doing that for a couple minutes, while you look up the number of your local indoor climbing gym, call them, and schedule a session. See how easy that was?

Until you try this, it may seem like a silly pursuit. I know it did to me. But once you're thirty feet up a wall, reaching for ever-smaller hand and foot holds, it all becomes quite clear. It's not about fitness or fear as much as it is about personal evaluation. When you reach a certain height in a climb, you'll reach a mental place you will probably not reach in any other fashion, as you ponder how willing you are to give up what you've gained, and how far you're willing to go.

42. Go hang gliding

Have you ever had a flying dream and awakened with a lingering sense of disappointment when you remembered you can't actually fly? Well, there's a solution! And the introduction to that solution can be much less terrifying than you imagine. Until I finally went on my first flight, I had all sorts of imagined scenarios for how one went about learning to hang glide. I knew you could fly tandem, but I still imagined leaping off a cliff, which was a daunting vision.

When I finally DID try it, the first flight was actually quite pleasant, because we were gently towed into the air behind a slow, ultralight aircraft. Before you know it, you're gently soaring through the sky, with an experienced pilot at the controls. And at the end of the flight, you'll probably be surprised to find yourself suddenly QUITE WILLING to make that more dramatic leap from a cliff for your first solo flight.

43. Walk in the rain

Ideally, this would be done in the nude, but your personal preferences and local ordinances may be an obstacle here. So make the best of it. When we say, "walk in the rain," we don't mean "in your Columbia rain gear" or "with an umbrella." Nooooo!!!! Wear something that feels good when wet and clinging to your skin. Let your hair get drenched and drip into your eyes! Jump in some puddles!

Strangely, all the prose and metaphors that reference feeling cleansed by the rain have a basis in reality. There are few things in life that are so easy to do, and have such an invigorating, refreshing effect. And as an adult, no one can yell at you when you get home soaking wet. And in a way, the best part comes AFTER a walk in the rain, when you warm yourself by a fire, or make some hot chocolate to take the chill away. Our planet is two-thirds water. You should get in touch with some once in a while.

44. Take a martial arts class

I imagine taking a martial arts class will also get you LITERALLY kicked in the ass on occasion, but the fact is that when pursued with the right teacher, and with the right attitude of discipline and commitment to the timeless values of an evolved martial art, the results will be as much a kick to the head as to the other end of your body. Few activities will hone your mind, spirit, and body in the way that focused martial arts study will. Plus, you can make sound effects!

45. Take a walk

No, taking a walk won't exactly "kick your ass into gear," but it will at least kick it out of your chair or wherever else it's planted. The minor increase in blood flow to the brain may lend some fresh air to your thoughts, and who knows — maybe you'll run into someone who will be pivotal to change in your life. You certainly won't meet anyone sitting in your office chair!

46. Go bungee jumping

Nobody ever gets hurt bungee jumping, right? No, seriously, are you sure? I mean, it seems like a long way down. What, I step through these straps? And fasten this? Are you sure it's gonna hold? What are you talking about? Hell no, I don't want my head to touch the water! Make sure that's tight. Step out here? You want me to count? Ten, nine, eight ... okay, put my feet right there ... seven, six, five .... hold my hands up? Oh, like a swan dive ... that's a long way down .... four, three, two, one ... aaaaaaaaaaaaaaaaaaaaaaaaaaaaaaaaaaaaaaaaa!

47. Go horseback riding

The next time you get in your car, ponder what it would be like if that thousand-pound-plus vehicle were ALIVE, and had some thoughts of its own about where it was going and when. Horseback riding may be a leisurely pastime for experienced riders, but your first ride is usually another story. Sitting astride a thousand pound creature that could easily kill you and learning how to make it do simple things like trotting, cantering, and stopping is an exercise in trust, confidence, and non-verbal communication that is like no other.

You'll build a special relationship as you get to know what "horsinality" means. Even a well-mannered, well-trained horse may be a little capricious and test your confidence by acting like it doesn't know what you want. It's amazingly courteous of these majestic creatures to let you climb up on their back in the first place; getting to know them a little is the least you could do, and is an experience like no other.

Play

48. Go fly a kite

The next time your pre-boomer generation boss or grandparent tells you to "go fly a kite," consider taking them up on it. If you live in a place that's never windy, it'll be great exercise. And if you live in a place where there IS wind, flying a kite can either be an adventure in craftsmanship and aerodynamics or a form of instant gratification, if you buy one ready to go. Either way, the end result has several small net benefits. First, it'll keep your chin up. Second, it'll expand your awareness of the world around you. And third, there are few things more meditative than pondering your connection with the sky once you've put something in it. After you've made a kite fly, give your dreams a try.

49. Bake something

This may not sound like something that will kick your ass, but this TOTALLY kicks MY ass every time I try it. Why? I love to cook, but HATE baking. Most of the cooking I enjoy is fusion or creative "ethnic" foods, especially things that require smart and artful prepping, a sense of timing and rhythm, and a searing hot pan. I like to see things take shape as I make them, sample a bit here and there to tweak things as I go, and juggle hot skillets and stuff. I like the evolution that occurs right before my eyes, and the ACTION.

But baking? Oh dear God. As a results-oriented perfectionist, nothing drives me more insane than the WAITING, especially knowing that if something was wrong, I won't know for thirty minutes, and if a cake layer is all flat and lifeless, I'll really just have to do it all over again. Baking now and then teaches me to slow down, pay attention, and most of all, be PATIENT, and let go. If all goes well, I can EAT CAKE. If not, I can go to the store and BUY CAKE. See? It's a win all around.

50. Do something you loved to do when you were a kid

This could be just about anything, now couldn't it. A few of my favorite pastimes as a kid included puddle-splashing and digging miniature rivers in the rain. They also included building model rockets, flying kites, riding a motorcycle, or just venturing out into the woods. When we're kids, we still understand one of the most important principles in life, which is that the most important thing is to be DOING something, and HAVING FUN doing it!

If you need to rediscover some of that feeling by engaging in a "childish" activity as an adult, GO FOR IT. Why do you think rock stars still seem so pleased with themselves in their fifties, even though they're losing their hair at the same rate that they're gaining a gut? Because they're in a band, man.

51. Buy a lotto ticket

Right. There's a reason they call it a "tax on the stupid", you know. Of thousands of successful people surveyed, do you know how many rank "luck" as an important key to their success? None. The top reasons offered are always persistence, recognizing opportunity, hard work, and a supportive partner. They say, "If you don't play, you won't win," but in this case, it would be more statistically accurate to say, "If you don't play, you won't LOSE".

52. Go golfing

Depending on your socio-economic values or political stance, you may find this idea revolting. Or silly, because you already hit the course today. If you fall into the former camp, DO IT NOW. You'll not only get outside whatever building you're in, you'll get outside your preconceptions, and learn things. Things like geometry and physics. Have you ever pondered how one degree in the position of your golf club translates to hundreds of feet left or right on the fairway?

Even if you just go to a driving range, the combination of focus and detachment required for a good swing will put parts of you to work that don't see much action otherwise. And who knows, maybe you'll make a business connection while also discovering that not only rich white guys play golf.

53. Go bowling

This is an activity that can challenge not only your sensibilities and coordination, but your olfactory inputs as well. Depending on what part of the country you live in, a bowling alley may be a clean and wholesome family recreation spot, or a frightening refuge for drifters and bikers that smells like hot dogs, ashtrays, and cheap beer. Either way, seize the day! You may find the idea of wearing someone else's shoes disgusting, but for one thing, they sanitize those things, and for another, stepping into someone else's shoes is the whole idea here.

If you find the idea of bowling unappealing because it brings back horrible memories of your lowbrow origins and your uncle Cletus, GET OVER IT and cut loose for a few hours. If it turns out you're horrible and have no style, make THAT your style. I embraced my "goofy foot" follow through and fast-pitch softball release with gusto, and bowled 132 on my first outing. I haven't joined the league or anything, but now I know that even though I won't score big in the tournament, I can score big with the laughs.

54. Listen to inspirational music

When we say "listen to inspirational music," this may conjure in your mind things like Handel's "Messiah" or Orff's "Carmina Burana," but this isn't necessarily what we mean. The Scots, for instance, always used music as they marched into battle. In fact, some would argue that it wasn't their painted faces, skirts, and fighting skills that drove the Romans from Britain, it was the bagpipes.

Sports teams always have fight songs, and the military has always used those annoying rhyming cadences to unify troops in training. "Fanfare for the Common Man" has been used for everything from TV coverage of the Olympics to vacuum cleaner sales conventions, and it seems like half the college and high school sports teams in the US use Journey's "Don't Stop Believing" as a crowd-rowser.

Personally, I can't clean the house without some rambunctious music at full blast, and if I ever need to get in a spiritual, reflective place, Arvo Pärt will do the trick every time. Need your ass kicked? Try some inspiring jams.

55. Go to a concert

Have you ever been to a concert that got you so jazzed up (sorry for the pun), that you stayed motivated and happy for a week? In 51 years I've probably been to 100 concerts, but some still move me years later when I think of them, including a classical koto concert in Tokyo, a Jefferson Starship concert in Detroit, a couple of operas, and a Sonny Rollins solo performance at the Michigan Union in Ann Arbor. The best concerts will reach you on a deep emotional level. Use the energy from those to keep you energized and motivated and, when the battery starts to die down, take a break. Later, when you need a little extra motivation, listen to a recording of the artist. That should amp you back up.

56. Take a half-day vacation

Go to Toronto, Seattle, or Dallas. Meet a friend. Find a coffee shop and spend the afternoon reading and chatting about architecture, science fiction movies, or something else you both enjoy. Drive home or hop on an airplane, as relaxed as you can remember being. Or don't. See if we care.

57. Go fishing

There are two totally different ways to approach this idea. If you're someone who works best by quietly stewing over an idea while doing something else, it might make sense to find a rowboat on a quiet lake somewhere and soak worms while your mind works on how to get moving on your goals.

On the other hand, if you're like me and you want to be totally overwhelmed by the moment so your conscious mind stops focusing on your mission, then you might need to go fly-fishing for salmon. When you're chest deep in freezing water with a fish the size of a German Shepherd leaping six feet over your head and Brown Bears thirty feet away taking a keen interest in the outcome of the battle, you probably won't be worrying about whether your brochure looks better with the text printed in Baskerville or Times New Roman.

58. Go into the changing room with a hot partner

The first time you try this it will seem really naughty. Especially if the sign says, "No going into the changing rooms with your hot partner." But if mom can go in with her kid to try on pants, why can't you go in with your sultry girlfriend? It'll save time since she doesn't have to come out to ask you what you think every two minutes. Or maybe it will cause you both to completely lose track of the time you spend in there.

59. Play "what I like about you" with your favorite person

Don't mess with this one. Seriously. This is one of the most powerful relationship builders we've ever experienced, and it can change your life or the life of someone you care about. In a group, ask each person to say one thing they like about the person across from them. It's more lasting if you write down what you like and give it to them on a slip of paper. In a love relationship, find a quiet place and take turns saying one thing you like about the other person. But bring Kleenex and condoms. It's that powerful.

60. Get the biggest bill you can afford and carry it around

Or even a bill you can't really afford. This idea is actually a riff on an idea we've talked about elsewhere, which is "Fake it 'Till You Make it," except that instead of trying to fool others about how rich or capable you are, you're trying to create the mindset of success in yourself. There are probably a lot of people who have never seen a $1000 bill (I hadn't until I did this exercise), so it could be really fun just to see one and cross that off your "Fuck it" list. But if you combine this idea with a few of the other ideas we've shared for getting you into the success mindset, you may feel enough of the feelings of accomplishment to get you over the hump.

61. Hug your inner child

Remember those times as a very young kid when you felt helpless and alone? Maybe you cried out for your parents and nobody came, or other kids teased you and you couldn't find a friend? The fear of feeling scared and alone may be keeping you from moving forward. One of the nicest things you can do for yourself is to find a quiet place, totally relax, and remember a time when you felt awful as a child. Then, with your adult, capable self, take the child in your arms and hold him or her tight and say, in a warm voice, "I love you. Everything's going to be alright. I will never leave you alone again."

Sacrifice

62. Make an amend

This may sound like something only people in AA would do, but ANYONE can benefit from making an amend, and anyone who thinks they don't owe anyone one needs to finally send in those sainthood applications, or prepare for their ascension or something.

Yes, we all leave a trail of damage behind us. Sometimes we don't realize it, and hilariously, sometimes we discover that in the places we thought we did the most damage, it wasn't even noticed. The classic example is the guy who spends hours tracking down that girl Suzie Smith he was so mean to in college, calls her, and says "Suzie, this is Bob Jones. I just wanted to say how sorry I am for all the mean things I said and did" and she replies "Bob WHO?"

This highlights another thing, which is that an apology is not an amends anyway. If you owe someone a hundred bucks and say "I'm sorry I never paid you that hundred bucks," that's an apology. An amends is when you actually give them the hundred bucks, and ALSO ask them if there's anything else you can do to help them out.

63. Teach someone else

One of the fastest ways to get your ass into gear is to stop thinking about your own problems and teach someone else. When you sincerely interest yourself in the welfare of others, wisdom and motivation arise independent of your self-interest. There are many, many reasons to teach other people. We can't possibly list them all, but here are a few: You'll add to the amount of good in the world. It's a chance to review what you know. You might discover that you can team up with your student. Your student might have some ideas that will help you. You might unknowingly train a future employee. You might remember a key concept that you'd forgotten.

64. Give away something of real value

Do you define yourself in terms of certain possessions? "I'm a BMW girl", you say, sniffing at the Hyundai behind you. This may be you, but I bet you've also noticed how liberating it is to get rid of a bunch of stuff. If you really want to shake up your self-concept and get moving, you can combine these concepts. Give away something you really value! Think of two or three possessions that you cling to. Is there anybody in your life who may need them more than you do? Give them those things at the first opportunity and just stop clinging to possessions as a way to keep from immersing yourself in life.

65. Fast

As in, don't eat.

We view almost everything we do through the lens of our experience, and eating is no exception. There's a good chance that you enjoy some things because you associate them with certain past experiences. If you could rearrange your days to create more time for effective work or use hunger as a motivation to get things done, what could you accomplish?

Seek Guidance

66. Get a mentor

Oh. You're ALREADY the best in the world at what you do? Sorry to waste your time. Feel free to get back to mentoring OTHER people. But if you're NOT the best in the world at what you do, then consider getting a mentor. If you think this idea is a waste of time, ponder this. Lance Armstrong had a mentor. It was five-time Tour de France winner Eddy Merckx. Actor Anthony Hopkins? Mentored by Sir Laurence Olivier. Martin Scorsese mentored Oliver Stone. Wolfgang Amadeus Mozart had Johann Christian Bach for a mentor. And who would Luke Skywalker be without Obi Wan?

We could keep listing great mentor relationships, but why don't you just GO GET ONE? Most fields these days have networks for connecting with mentors, but you can simply ask someone you respect if they'd consider this kind of relationship. Still uncomfortable with the idea? Then DON'T CALL IT MENTORING. Just ask that person out to lunch, and start picking their brain and/or modeling yourself after the traits they possess that you respect or admire.

A mentor relationship can take many forms, but whatever shape it takes, you will know when it's working. You'll have a heightened sense of awareness of the worthiness and sensibilities of your pursuits, and spend a lot less time second-guessing your reasoning and motives, because you will have objectified them with someone you trust and respect.

67. Ask for help

Pride is over-rated. A couple of years ago, I was in a jam. My business had hit a flat spot, and a house-sitting gig fell through at the last minute. It would be about a month before my cash flow would open up, and I had no idea what to do. I was really in a bit of a panic for a couple of weeks.

When I shared my dilemma with an old friend, he said "have you asked anyone for help?" and I busted out laughing as I said "No. I don't ask people for help. THEY ask ME for help." But his point was well-taken. Later that day, I reluctantly called a friend and business associate with whom I have a long and trusted history. I was REALLY uncomfortable as I dialed. I was about to ask someone for a spontaneous personal loan of two or three grand!.

I explained my situation to this friend, and he said "so what do you really need?" and I said "A place to live and some cash fast." He said, "I just had a nice little apartment open up, you can move in this weekend. We'll work out the money whenever. What else?" I was a little aghast. "Well now that THAT'S out of the way, about seven or eight hundred bucks." He replied "No problem. What else?" I was totally blown away. I had been freaking out for a week, and one phone call, humbling myself a little, and BAM. Problem solved. Anxiety gone. And this interaction actually strengthened our relationship. The lesson? Pride sucks, and humility is really okay. You'll be amazed at how much people LIKE helping people, and everyone benefits a little. Need help? We all do now and then. Go ahead and ask.

68. Hire a coach

You know how when Olympics gold medal winners step down from the pedestal after the ceremony and go hug some more or less anonymous person in a track suit, and maybe cry or do a snoopy dance? That's their COACH, without whom they wouldn't have that hefty medal around their neck and millions of dollars of endorsement offers awaiting them.

You wouldn't enter a boxing ring or run an NFL team without a coach, so in today's competitive world, why run your LIFE without one? I used to scoff at the idea of a "Life Coach"; to me it sounded like some mamby-pamby new age figure that would spout philosophical drivel that I probably already knew. And then a friend paid for a few sessions with one, and I got my butt kicked. A good life coach will help you quickly assess your situation, and jump into action with strategies to enhance it. The most successful people you encounter have probably consulted one. Why go into the life's battles without a trainer and strategist? Free up all that self-analysis time so you can DO STUFF.

69. Take a class about it

With the thousands of affordable community colleges at our disposal, I'm amazed we're not all in school ALL THE TIME. In my community, a single class for a full semester costs less than dinner for two at a fine restaurant! Putting this idea to work changed my life. I was a late bloomer with computers. The desktop computer rose to prominence as I was finishing school, so I avoided work that required solid computer skills for years. I joked that I was waiting for them to get to the point where they operated with voice commands.

Finally, in 1999, I broke down and realized this wasn't happening any time soon, and took an "Intro to Computers" class. After just a few weeks, I had a shocking revelation. All those people around me who I thought knew how to use computers? They have NO IDEA what they're doing much of the time, and muddle through, ashamed to admit it. The following semester, I took a basic HTML class. My assigned class partner was 17 year-old that knew more than the instructor. I asked him how he had learned so much, and he said "on the internet." I took his cue, and several months later was designing websites well enough to make a living from it, and quit my waiter job.

70. Go to a motivational event

Are you a hater when it comes to motivational speakers? You think those guys are all full of crap? Or that they get you all charged up but the feeling doesn't last? Listen, with all due respect, being cynical is one reason you haven't done anything great lately! If someone can help you get highly motivated, even for a day, then doesn't the part about turning that motivation into action kinda fall on your shoulders?

We've attended or watched recordings of most of the great motivators of the past 30 years, and even if you don't invent the new Facebook the instant you leave their seminars, they almost always provide you with an energy boost and a few good ideas for improving your business or personal life. If you haven't ever been to a motivational event, you owe it to yourself to try it once. It could be just the thing you need to kick your ass into gear.

71. Read a book about it

I love business books. I read about two per week and there are good ideas in almost every one. The closer the subject matter of the book is to an issue I'm working on, the more useful the book is (thank you Mr. Obvious). Several times I've outlined the contents of a book and found that, by following my outline, I've been able to work through a problem or create a new system, much to the benefit of my investors.

72. Copy an existing version

We've written elsewhere about following an existing plan or reading a book about the problem you're facing. This is an even more straightforward suggestion: just copy an existing version of the thing you're trying to do. If you want to be the next Google, figure out what they're doing to deliver search engine results, and do that.

Two major "watch-outs!" – one, this suggestion is for DEVELOPING a new product, service, building, video, or whatever. Make sure your finished product is different enough so that you don't run into any copyright infringement issues. Two, you're smart, creative and ambitious, so once your ass has gotten into gear, use your brains and talent to figure out how to personalize your version. The world has enough bad copies!

Take Action

73. Go to a cafe and start your business

This idea is nothing new. Back when newspapers were a new thing, and the Dutch Trading Company was the world's FEDEX, cafes were THE place to stay hip to the latest business trends, do commerce, and make deals.

Three of my successful ventures were born in a cafe. The right coffee shop is a fantastic place for ideas to brew. You can isolate and focus or be social. A good caffeine-jacked barrista might give your brain a bump it needs, and if not, there's an endless supply of caffeine to give your OWN brain a bump. Not only is a cafe a great place to brainstorm and plan, but you can even RUN a business from a cafe, especially if you're in a community that has one of the increasingly popular "community-office-space-and-cafe" locations. What are you waiting for? If you need a break, you can take this book with you!

74. Do something that doesn't cost anything

The other day a friend of mine took his wife and kids to the movies. He said it was a great flick, but hardly worth the 83 bucks. No joke. It seems like a lot of small daily decisions are shaped by the likely cost.

Where to have lunch? You'd love to go to that new sushi place, but it's so darn expensive. It would be great to go to the ball game, but after gas, parking, tickets and concessions, you may as well have bought opera tickets. It's not surprising services like Netflix are becoming so popular.

But why not get all the things you want and not pay for it? Nah, we're not suggesting you "dine and dash" at your local five-star restaurant, but why not go to a local rec-league game? Hit a local gallery that doesn't charge admission? Most towns these days have a plethora of events daily that don't cost anything. Look at your local listings and try one!

75. Paint that room

Especially if you're a homeowner, there's a reasonably good chance that there's some room in your house that you've designated as a study, guest room, or some other kind of special-purpose room. And there's an equally good chance that at some point you started using it as an all-purpose storage room or "way station," thinking "I'll just put this stuff here until I paint this room," then leaving both actions on the backburner.

This kind of thing is directly reflective of certain corners of our mind where we do the same thing, linking one activity to another and doing neither. Why not get your butt in gear and finally paint it? Doing so will activate all sorts of things in your brain among other things. Will it be a light airy room? A dynamically color-themed room? A place with dark walls where you can brood? You'll figure all these things out while you organize and discard the crap in your way, and maybe experience a similar clearing of the mind in the process!

76. Make your own list of 101 things to kick your ass into gear

Hey, I don't know you, so I have NO IDEA what will really kick your ass into gear. But even asking the question "what are X number of things that will kick my ass into gear?" is a good start toward kicking it into gear. Start with a short list if you need to. Maybe ten things. And then go do ONE of them.

77. Start a salon

No, not a hair or nail salon, that old-fashioned kind where people gather and talk about interesting things, and meet interesting people. There are lots of "networking" events these days, but they all seem to have a corporate flavor, and although great contacts can be made this way, there's always an undercurrent of the friendships having some "purpose." Getting a classic salon rolling takes skill; I've watched several friends try it, and it's very easy for these events to devolve into just being a party or coffee klatsch. Give it a go. Who knows, maybe you'll accidentally create the Algonquin Round Table of the 21st Century or something!

78. Absolutely refuse to do anything

This works for two-year-olds, so why not give it a try yourself? You'll notice a few things right away. First of all, refusing to do things that people ask or tell you to do will quickly redefine some boundaries. Which is exactly why most two-year olds are so fond of the word "no." Saying no to someone is a great way to test their resolve, and examine the real motives behind their request. Is the request reasonable, as in "honey, I just cleaned the house, packed the kids' lunches for the week, and have dinner almost ready, would you mind taking out the garbage?", or is it insane, like "I don't CARE if your labor pains just started, get in that kitchen and bake me a pie!"

Aside from these more obvious aspects of refusing to do anything, you may discover something surprising. It is incredibly hard to actually not do ANYTHING. In fact, it doesn't occur to most people that yoga, for instance, originally evolved to help a person who needed to be still to actually do so. Try sitting on the floor in just about any position you like, but without moving. I mean REALLY not moving. Not only does the body constantly twitch slightly just to maintain balance, you find that almost no part of your body enjoys being completely still unless you're sleeping. Try being a worthless do-nothing for just a day. It may rock your world. By the way, sleeping doesn't count. That's actually doing something.

79. Plan a trip around the world

One thing I've noticed about trips around the world is that I don't take them if I don't plan them. I've barely scratched the surface myself; I've only been to Canada, Mexico, 39 of the 50 states, the Netherlands, and Kenya. Clearly I still have a lot of ground to cover. And nothing will kick your ass quite like planning and paying for, dreaming about, and then actually EXPERIENCING a trip to somewhere you've never been. Don't have a big budget? Do it in baby steps. Just do one country. Or if you're young enough, join the Peace Corp or an NGO, or join the Army. At least PREPARE for the trip. Get a passport if you don't have one. It's amazing how once you DO have one, you want to get it stamped. And if you're American, don't forget to dress like a Canadian.

80. Employ Caffeine

Are you telling me nobody's written about this? How can that be? What could be more obvious than the idea of getting hopped up on caffeine and getting your ass kicked into gear? One cup of coffee helps me wake up in the morning, but that second cup really gets me to the edge. I'm sharper. I have more creative ideas, I see right past obstacles, and the words just seem to flow right out. And that third cup, well, come on! You wanna see someone get organized and start to produce, that's me on three cups of coffee. Most of my best ideas have come under the influence, so to speak, of caffeine, and if you want to hear more, just stop in at my local coffee shop, buy me a cup or four, and I'll talk your ear off for as long as you care to listen!

81. Organize your office

I'm always telling people that if you don't find or create a system for common tasks, you'll severely limit your potential. I only say it because it's true – doing the same thing over and over again without thinking about how to streamline the work will put a creative person into a slump. Systematizing is just making sure that your tasks are set up to be as efficient as possible. So start with your office. Make sure you have enough desk space to comfortably review and sign documents. Make sure you have an out box or a file cabinet close enough to reach without standing up. Make sure your wastebasket is within easy reach and that you put a LOT of stuff in there.

82. Make that decision

How many times in life do we end up doing something poorly or not doing it at all because we haven't resolved an inner conflict? For me, it was once very frequent. I admit I once struggled with the idea of success, probably because I was raised in a family that equated financial success with shallowness. I now know that's nonsense, but my first reaction to many situations used to keep me from success. Is there an inner conflict that keeps from you performing as well as you could? We suggest doing everything you can to get it resolved. Try therapy, bungee jumping, meditation, success coaching, shouting a lot, and working your butt off. Once you get past that internal barrier, your performance and results will skyrocket.

83. Ready, fire, aim!

We call this "The Dick Cheney Theory of Getting Things Done." Just don't do it with actual firearms! But sometimes in business it's better to fire first and adjust your aim later. Get started and avoid the paralysis of shooting for perfection.

This is especially true if you can measure your results. One example is in online advertising. If you want more people to visit your website, create two ads without worrying too much about getting 'em both perfect. Pay attention to which one gets you more visitors and make two ads like that one. Do it again and again. Your aim will improve as you apply what you've learned.

84. Don't just do something, DO SOMETHING!

Small results are hard to measure. If you do something right but it's small, you may need a microscope to figure out if it helped you. But if you do something big, you're going to know if it worked. And if it didn't, you should be able to see what didn't work about it. Just don't do something crazy just to be doing something! You have to clearly identify your goal and the path that will get you there, but once you've got that, we're sure you can find SOME significant action to get you started.

85. Work to learn

Looking for that perfect job? Stop! It doesn't exist. You're wasting time that could be spent learning. There are so many skills needed to be really successful, whether you're working for someone else or running your own business.

It's a huge waste of time to work just for the money. Everybody with high aspirations should know how to do these seven things: listen well, delay personal gratification, read people's emotions, write well, sell, organize, and inspire others. All other skills are specialties. Find a job that can teach you one or more of the things you need to do the stuff you want to do when you grow up. If a job teaches you to be outstanding at one or more of them, you should be willing to work there for free. Just don't tell your boss!

86. Compete

I'm very competitive, I admit it. I'm probably a lot more competitive than you, but if you are half as competitive as me and you want something to kick your ass into gear, get into competition with somebody. It can be a lot of fun, especially if you tend to win, like me. Hey, you can say to a friend, I bet I can apply for more jobs this week than you can. Call a business associate and tell her that you are going to create three new advertising campaigns for your business. Can she do as many? If your mentor runs a business, share your gross income for last month with him and see who can create the largest percentage increase next month. In the end, both people win because you'll both have fun, learn some things, and hopefully increase your income.

87. Cooperate

I can be very cooperative if I think we can help each other. I'm probably as cooperative as anybody, so if you are half as cooperative as me and you want something to kick your ass into gear, find somebody who can help you get things done, and offer to help them get some of their things done. Cooperating can be a lot of fun and is almost always a win-win situation. Hey, you can say to a friend, I know you're looking for a job, so I'll send over everything I find that might work for you. Can you do the same for me? Call a business associate and tell her that you are going to create a new advertising campaign for your business and you'd like some advice. Is there anything she'd like advice on? If your mentor also runs a business, share your gross income for last month with one another, and see if you can come up with a good plan to increase one another's gross for next month. Both people win because both will have fun, learn some things, and almost certainly increase their income.

88. Take the first step

So you know what you want to achieve and you've laid out the major steps to achieve it. You've got the tools and the know-how in place and a calendar set for the major steps. You're excited about the project and you know you should get going, but somehow you just can't get started. Would it help if we told you this is actually a very common problem? Didn't think so. We suspect it's related to the fact that your mind can't help but see the entire project laid out in front of you and the sheer amount of work seems overwhelming.

We suggest that you resolve to take only the first step today. The first step and absolutely nothing more. Tell yourself, "once I get this done, I will do no more on this project today," and stick to it. Suddenly you'll be free of the burden of trying to complete the entire project and happy because once you've spent the two hours or whatever it takes to get the first step done, you can go to the golf course or play with your three-year old. That's what I'm about to do.

89. Find the perfect environment

If you've spent any part of your life working, creating, or studying, you've probably noticed that you work a lot better in certain settings. Some folks like absolute quiet; I like a fair amount of sound in my working environment. Some folks like a cool office; I like to be sweating a bit when I work. Don't know why, that's just how it is.

Overall, I suggest thinking about seven factors in your environment: amount of light, amount and type of sound, temperature, presence of other people, caffeine level, type and comfort level of seat or footwear, and tools.

Just for the record, here are my preferences: lots of light from the computer screen but very little in the room; opera or other emotional music, rather loud; warmer than room temperature; no people unless I'm at a coffee shop, in which case I want it packed and noisy; caffeine level well above average; padded office chair with wheels; and a big flat-screen monitor powered by Macintosh.

90. Ask yourself, "What is one thing I can do right now?" Then do it.

You know that project you've been meaning to do? What is one thing you could do on it right now? Forget about whether there is something you'll have to do after the one thing. Just do the one thing and make sure you stop immediately when it's done.

I've noticed that when I try to think too globally, I often end up planning more than doing. Not that there's anything wrong with planning, but there are some folks out there who can just up and get started. By the time I've begun, they're half done. My illusions about creating something better won't hold up very well if I never get anything done. And you can't take the second step unless you take the first. So find the first step and take it.

91. Do everything you can think of, even if it doesn't have anything to do with the thing you want to get done

Are you frozen by the thought of taking that first step on your new project? Are there too many things lurking around undone to allow you to focus on the most important task? What you need, my friend, is momentum. It's time to get moving, so just start doing stuff. There's only one critical rule for this task – whatever you do, you have to be DOING something. No introspective tasks allowed – no reading, no sitting and listening to music, no soaking in the tub.

Open the first three envelopes on your desk and file the papers away. Pay a bill or two. Empty the trash. Take those shirts off the laundry hangers and hang them on your chrome ones. Clean your monitor screen. Pluck your eyebrows. Once you're fully in motion, take the first tiny step toward your goal and see where it takes you. If you've had enough caffeine, you'll probably get a lot farther than you think!

92. Pay someone to do the part you don't like

There's no reason to do tasks you don't like! Divide your goals into clearly defined tasks, and find someone on the internet to do them. Virtual assistants will work for as little as $4/hour. One of my business clients works for a demanding Fortune 500 company. When he absolutely has to get away from work but has a deadline, he uses his virtual assistant. When I see him at the gym he's always smiling. "I'm working," he says. "when I get back to the office, there'll be a report in my email. I look like an F-ing genius!" I know that's annoying, but it's a LOT less annoying when you're the one saying it.

93. Count your blessings

When was the last time you counted your blessings? I mean really paid attention to all the good things in your life? You've got 'em, alright. I bet I can even guess a few of them. Like, you can read. And understand what you're reading. And you aspire ... to something. That's why you're reading this book, right? Or, if a friend recommended it to you, you have friends, which is one of biggest blessings I know of. And at least enough leisure time to read. And if you're one of the many, many people who have far more than the basic blessings, remember how you got a few of 'em. Could you do it again? I'm sure of it. Just get started.

94. Create a personal creed

At my dojo we have a kids creed. It starts with: "I am committed to be the best I can possibly be. I believe that attitude matters. I will focus on the positive and overcome the negative." We say it out loud and with huge gestures in every class. If you've never done this kind of affirmation you may not realize how powerful it can be. Our kids are so positively charged after the creed they feel like they can do almost anything. For that matter, so do our instructors. If you had a personal creed, what would it be?

95. Fix it yerself, dangit!

We all have something around the house that needs fixing. Maybe it's a computer problem, or a piece of furniture, or something minor with the car that we keep procrastinating around. Here's an idea - choose something that you don't know how to fix, and fix it! Between the internet and the thousands of repair guides in book form out there, it's almost certain that there's a detailed guide for fixing it.

We're talking mostly about physical objects here, but why limit yourself. We all have broken or poorly-performing relationships in both our personal and professional lives, why not fix one of them? Aside from the personal gratification that usually accompanies solving a problem, maybe you'll save a few bucks too!

Visualize

96. Make a dream list

I've never cared much for the idea of a "bucket list." Why frame your entire list with the idea of death? To me this offers even more opportunity for procrastination: "Well, I'll certainly do this before I DIE, so why worry about it TODAY?" Make a list of dreams and aspirations. Do it with no initial restrictions on practicality. Have fun first. It's just a list. What would you be doing today, if you could be doing anything you wanted in the world? Cool. Now get to work on it!

97. Find photos of people you want to emulate

I had never tried this until Nick suggested it for this book, but it's bloody brilliant. You may already be familiar with the idea of keeping a picture around as a visualization tool for goals, but this was exceptionally thought-provoking, and FUN. I pretty quickly realized I didn't want to LOOK like a lot of the people I'd like to emulate; I mean – nothing personal gentleman – but Gandhi, Warren Buffet, and Stanley Kubrick aren't especially handsome fellows. So I threw in George Clooney. It's okay to want to emulate someone's LOOKS too, right? But seriously, this was an engaging way to think about whom you admire. And taping Warren Buffet and George Clooney's faces next to my monitor remind me that my dashing looks don't pay the bills.

98. List all the good things that will result from doing it

Maybe one reason you're having trouble getting started is because you haven't taken the time to clearly visualize all the good things that might come from getting that task done. A vague notion that your life will be better if you write that novel you've always dreamed of usually won't motivate you very much. But a concrete list of the good that might come from it, from the most mundane to the most outrageous, could really get you pumped up.

Suppose your one big idea is a novel. If you get it written, at least you'll get it off your to-do list. You could share it with your friends. An agent might like it enough to take it on. Maybe it will get accepted at a big publishing house. If the screen rights get optioned, you might get enough money to build that lake house you've always wanted. Maybe Ellen Degeneres will have you on her show and your movie will take off, making you richer than Paris Hilton. You could cast Beyonce in the starring role, and get invited to Tiger Woods' yacht, where you can hit golf balls into the Caribbean Sea while you sip the rarest Japanese green tea over glacier ice.

99. List all the bad things that will result from not doing it

Maybe one reason you're having trouble getting started is because you haven't taken the time to clearly visualize all the bad things that might come from never getting that task done. A vague notion that your life will be worse if you never write that novel usually won't motivate you very much. But a concrete list of the bad that might come from it, from the most mundane to the most outrageous, could really get you off your seat cushion.

Suppose your one big idea is a novel. If you never get it written, you'll never get it off your to-do list. You'll never be able to share it with your friends, and they'll continue to think you're full of crap. An agent will never have the chance to see it, and will never take it on. It will never get accepted at a big publishing house, and the screen rights will never get optioned. You'll continue to be stuck working at the copy shop, making copies of other people's projects and taking smoke breaks behind the dumpster. You'll have to content yourself with your collection of People magazines, reading at night about celebrities like Paris Hilton, Beyonce, and Tiger Woods and drinking second-rate chamomile tea from that cup you "borrowed" from the Red Roof Inn.

100. Promise yourself a reward

I don't feel like writing this article right now, but I'd love a cookie! Okay, you can have a cookie, but not until you write the article.

But I don't want to write the article! Okay, then at least outline the darn thing. Oh, alright. The idea is that you can get yourself to do small tasks by promising yourself a reward. You just need to follow the discipline of sticking to the promise. If you can do that, you can pair big rewards with big accomplishments. It's a great way to motivate yourself.

By the way, you can have that cookie now.

101. Ask "What if?"

Looking for a new direction in life? Stuck on a problem? Try asking "what if?" You know, like "what if I had a million dollars" or "what if I could go anywhere I wanted right now?" or "what if I could be with anyone I liked at the moment?" Would you invest the million? Give it away? Would you want to be where you are, or somewhere else? Would you want to be with your loved one, or someone different?

Asking "what if" not only opens up your mind to possibilities, it clarifies what you're unhappy about with your existing situation. And when working on problems or creative ventures, "what if" lets you stop focusing on the problem, and start dreaming up solutions. I often reference something Einstein said about this, which is "Problems cannot be solved by the same level of thinking that created them". So, what if you made that "what if" list RIGHT NOW?

Appendix (Butt List)

aft
arse
ass
backside
badonkadonk
behind
biscuits
booty
bottom
bum
bunda (Brazil)
butt
caboose
cakes
can
cheeks
culo (Spanish)
derrière
duff
fanny
glutes
heinie
keester
patootie
pooper
posterior
rear
rear-end
rump
seat
stern
tail
tail feathers
tuchis (Yiddish)
tush

About the Authors

Ian Gray is a media consultant, writer, musician, and budding public speaker with an eye on becoming the next Ellen.

Nicklaus Suino is a martial arts expert, attorney, writer, and business consultant who specializes in kicking your ass into gear.

Read more at kickyourass101.com